HAND SHADOW FUN

Verses by
Frank Jacobs

Illustrations by
Henry Bursill

DOVER PUBLICATIONS, INC.
Mineola, New York

Bibliographical Note

Hand Shadow Fun, first published by Dover Publications, Inc., in 2015, is a republication in a new format of *Fun with Hand Shadows,* first published by Dover in 1996. It is comprised of a selection of illustrations by Henry Bursill, originally published in *Hand Shadows to be Thrown Upon the Wall* (1859) and *Hand Shadows: Second Series* (1860) by Griffith and Farran, London. The accompanying verses were written specially for this edition by Frank Jacobs.

International Standard Book Number

ISBN-13: 978-0-486-79674-1
ISBN-10: 0-486-79674-4

Manufactured in the United States by LSC Communications
79674408   2019
www.doverpublications.com

HAND SHADOWS

An ancient pastime that has lost none of its ability to amuse, the creation of hand shadows is simple. Position your hands as indicated in the illustrations shown in this book, put a source of light behind them and cast the shadows onto the blank part of a wall.

To add to the fun, Frank Jacobs has written new nonsense verses to go with each traditional shadow.

HAND
SHADOW
FUN

THE GOOSE

A stupid goose
Has gotten loose.
No, not a moose—
A goose named Bruce.
The people holler, "What's the use?
"We'll never catch a goose that's loose!"
But look! A hand is holding Bruce—
A hand that grips him like a noose,
Which means we've gotten back our goose—
At least till Bruce
Again gets loose.

THE GOOSE

THE DEER

The deer we see here is a buck;
His antlers tell us so.
In mating season, with some luck,
He'll find himself a doe.
Let's hope he hasn't long to wait,
That soon she will appear—
And when he says, "Please be my mate,"
She'll answer, "Yes, my deer."

THE DEER

THE BUNNY

This pesky bunny comes to feast
  On lettuce in your garden.
You'd think that once or twice, at least,
  He'd say, "I beg your pardon."

THE BUNNY

BIRDS

When planning a vacation trip,
Birds need no plane, or train or ship
To take them to some far-flung destination;
They spread their wings and fly for free,
Which means they never have to see
A travel agent for a reservation.

BIRDS

THE GOAT

Although they give us milk and cheese,
Most goats are rather hard to please;
They're rough and gruff, won't take advice—
In other words, they just aren't nice.
And even when we treat them well,
They still give off that dreadful smell.
Should one show up, be on your guard;
Don't get too close—he'll butt you hard.

THE GOAT

11

TOBY

Toby was a happy dog;
Toby never growled.
Toby was a quiet dog
who never yelped or howled.
Toby never tore around;
Toby always sat,
until that dreadful day last week
when we brought home a cat.

TOBY

THE ELEPHANT

The elephant's no household pet;
   He doesn't bark or purr;
He's so gigantic, you can bet
   That lions call him "Sir."
Most times he is a peaceful soul
   Who seldom starts a riot.
But get him mad? Well, on the whole,
   I don't think you should try it.

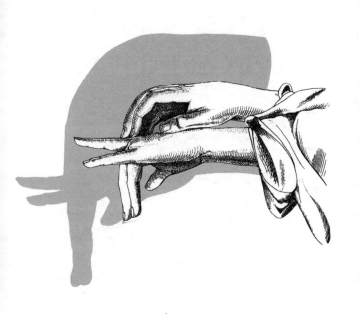

THE ELEPHANT

THE GREYHOUND

Because he is so sleek and trim,
　The greyhound runs quite fast;
The other dogs won't race with him—
　They know they'd finish last.

THE GREYHOUND

THE PIG

If pigs were human, they would go
    To restaurants and delis;
The only pleasure that they know
    Is filling up their bellies.
But should a skinny pig you find
    Who's hard to feed and fatten,
A word from you will change his mind
    When spoken in pig Latin.

THE PIG

THE BRUIN

The bruin, with his teeth and paws,
Does not obey our local laws.
So if you see one walking past,
Just say "Hello"—and run real fast!

THE BRUIN

GUESS WHO?

Who is this creature that we see?
   It's clear he's not an ox;
He's surely not a chimpanzee,
   A kangaroo or fox.
But if you said a mule he is,
   You got the answer right;
Not only have you solved the quiz—
   You're also pretty bright.

GUESS WHO?

THE OLD GROWLER

This bulldog, many people say,
  Once filled his foes with fright.
But now that he is old and gray,
  He'd rather growl than fight.

THE OLD GROWLER

A FRIGHTENED MAN

The fellow pictured here
Is quivering with fear.
You can see that he is shaken to the core;
It seems he caught a glimpse—
This wimpiest of wimps—
Of that old, gray growler on the page before.

A FRIGHTENED MAN

THE TORTOISE

Just hear the tortoise boast out loud
  While speeding down the trail.
He's got good reason to be proud—
  He just outraced a snail.

THE TORTOISE

A BOY

Who is this boy? It could be Roy,
  Or Jack, or Jim or Harry;
It might be John or Algernon
  Or maybe Sam or Larry.
We've tried our best; we've guessed and
    guessed
  A dozen times this week.
We've still no clue; I guess it's true
  That shadows never speak.

A BOY

THE CAMEL

The grouchy camel, as a rule,
Is twice as stubborn as a mule.
He hates to work; he's often rude—
In short, he's got an attitude.
He tries all sorts of nasty tricks—
He spits and grunts and whines and kicks;
He hates the desert, hates the sun;
He hates all humans, every one.
Oh, by the way, 'twixt me and you,
He hates all other camels too.

THE CAMEL

SHAKESPEARE

Will Shakespeare must have spent his days
  A very busy fellow
To write so many famous plays
  Like *Hamlet* and *Othello;*
He worked for weeks without a break
  With great determination.
Let's hope he found the time to take
  At least a small vacation.

SHAKESPEARE

THE HARE

Some people have the habit
To call a hare a rabbit,
While others may declare
A rabbit is a hare.
It's up to you to choose
The name you wish to use;
The rabbit doesn't care,
And neither does the hare.

THE HARE

MIKE

Mike lost the only pig he had
Just yesterday, which made him sad.
How come he's now a happy guy?
Just turn the page and you'll know why.

MIKE

MIKE'S PIG

Hooray! Let's shout it loud and clear!
Mike's pig's been found, so give a cheer!
You'll see his shadow on the wall;
I guess he wasn't lost at all.

MIKE'S PIG

THE COCKATOO

Because of his enormous crest,
The cockatoo can be a pest;
Each day he prances 'round his nest
And flaunts his crest from east to west.
The other birds are not impressed;
They kind of wish he'd take a rest.

THE COCKATOO

THE SAGE

This gent has reached a ripe old age
And now is famous as a sage,
Which means that he is wise, you see,
And brainy as a man can be.
And that is why we take to heart
That growing old can make us smart
(Though some men, it is sad to say,
Grow up as fools and stay that way.)

THE SAGE

THE BULL

The bull, to say the very least,
Can be a most ferocious beast;
When angry, he may use his horns to gore you.
And that is why it makes good sense
To duck behind a tree or fence
Whenever there's a bull who's heading for you.

THE BULL

THE SQUIRREL

The squirrel leaps from limb to limb—
An exercise that keeps him slim.
Maybe you and I should try it—
Then we'd never need to diet.

THE SQUIRREL

THE EAGLE

Above the treetops, soaring high,
You'll see the mighty eagle.
With wings outspread, he rules the sky—
No bird is quite so regal.
Today the eagle has become
The symbol of our nation,
So sound the trumpet, beat the drum
And start the celebration!

THE EAGLE

MRS. GAMP

"Just who on earth is Mrs. Gamp?
She's not on any postage stamp.
We know she doesn't live next door,
Or run the local candy store.
We doubt that she's a movie star
Or drives a very fancy car.
Who can she be? It's hard to say;
We asked, but she yelled, 'Go away!'"

MRS. GAMP

SHEEP

I'm told some folks are counting sheep
At night when they can't fall asleep.
With this in mind, we should discuss
If sheep at night are counting us.

SHEEP

THE SWAN

The swan can swim while sitting down,
Yet stays afloat and doesn't drown.
In many ways it seems a shame
That you and I can't do the same.

THE SWAN